essentials

Making Great Presentations

Time-saving books that teach specific skills to busy people, focusing on what really matters; the things that make a difference – the *essentials*. Other books in the ESSENTIALS series include:

Writing Good Reports

Speaking in Public

Responding to Stress

Succeeding at Interviews

Solving Problems

Hiring People

Getting Started on the Internet

Writing Great Copy

Making the Best Man's Speech

Feeling Good for No Reason

Making the Most of Your Time

For full details please send for a free copy of the latest catalogue. See back cover for address.

The things that really matter about

Making Great Presentations

Ghassan Hasbani

ESSENTIALS

First published in 1999 by
How To Books Ltd, 3 Newtec Place,
Magdalen Road, Oxford OX4 1RE, United Kingdom
Te: (01865) 793806   Fax: (01865) 248780
email: info@howtobooks.co.uk
www.howtobooks.co.uk

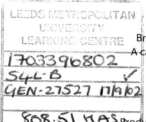

British Library Cataloguing in Publication Data.
A catalogue record for this book is available from
the British Library.

Editing by Diana Brueton
Cover design by Shireen Nathoo Design
Produced for How To Books by Deer Park Productions
Typeset by Euroset, Alresford, Hampshire
Printed and bound in the United Kingdom

NOTE: The material contained in this book is set out in good faith for
general guidance and no liability can be accepted for loss or expense
incurred as a result of relying in particular circumstances on
statements made in the book. Laws and regulations are complex and
liable to change, and readers should check the current position with
the relevant authorities before making personal arrangements.

ESSENTIALS *is an imprint of*
How To Books

Contents

Preface

Employers today look for people with good communication skills. In general, people are becoming better at communicating, and presentation skills are becoming a significant part of any vocational training. Yet still, many people find it difficult to convey an idea to an audience or to convince others with certain ideas. Many are also too nervous to present effectively. If you are one of those people, or an executive who made it through the ranks but still feels nervous about presenting, this concise book will give you the key techniques which will enable you to become a more confident presenter. By the end of a train journey or a short flight, you will know much more about presenting techniques than you do now.

Whether you are preparing for a presentation or are about to give one and want some last minute tips, you will find this book invaluable. Nowadays, we spend a great deal of time in presentations and people expect to get value for their money. A presentation for one hour, with an audience of five people could cost a company anything between two hundred and a few thousand pounds if we include the accommodation costs, salaries and travel expenses. You will not succeed in capturing the interest of many people if your presentation is not perceived to add value to them.

A good presentation reflects well on the presenter, so I hope this book will help you achieve your personal and career goals by highlighting the techniques. Enjoy reading it.

Ghassan Hasbani
B.Eng(Hons), MBA, C.Eng., MIEE

1 Creating Your Own Style

Being liked and trusted is about having charisma.
Having charisma comes from having a style.

4

things that
really matter

1 **COMMUNICATING AT THE RIGHT LEVEL**

2 **SELECTING THE RIGHT STYLE**

3 **USING EFFECTIVE BODY LANGUAGE**

4 **TAKING CONTROL**

Presentations are very powerful communication tools and can work to your advantage as well as disadvantage. The style with which you present has a great importance in the success of your presentation. The trick is to find the style that **suits your personality** and **fits the situation**. You will undoubtedly have to present in a multitude of situations. If your style is always formal, you may find it hard to reach your audience in an informal setting. Your style should reflect your personality as closely as possible. However, sometimes you need to employ certain techniques to adapt to the situation and deliver your message effectively. Actors, for example, don't always play parts that fully reflect their personalities, but they employ techniques to get the part right, adding a personal touch to it. You can therefore see personal characteristics of an actor in both the villain and the virtuous roles.

Employing certain techniques can help you give a suitable performance at the right occasion.

IS THIS YOU?

● *I was taught to present in one way but it doesn't seem to work all the time.* ● *People don't always seem interested in what I am presenting.* ● *I find it difficult to stand still when I present.* ● *People in the audience start talking to each other, ignoring me completely.* ● *My boss keeps enquiring about progress but doesn't seem to be interested when I give a detailed presentation at team meetings.*

(1) COMMUNICATING AT THE RIGHT LEVEL

The way you talk is a major contributor to the style of your presentation. Although you should be yourself and talk as you normally do, you may tend to put on an artificial accent and behaviour when put under pressure. To be yourself under these conditions is easier said than done.

In order to reach the required degree of confidence and relaxation, it is necessary to train and prepare yourself before you face the audience. Once the training and rehearsals are completed, you feel more confident to think about what you want to say, as you do not have to worry about the way you say it.

The style with which you present largely depends on the way you normally talk. Some presenters talk as if they are reading from a newspaper, without any emphasis, pauses or body movements. This can grab the audience's attention for a very short period, after which their interest in the presentation will rapidly fade. Some presenters can be so monotonous that their audience find it difficult to stay awake. Going to the other extreme may not be suitable either. You need to find the level at which your audience would like you to communicate with them, then find the right balance between the extremes and employ techniques which ensure that your audience maintains their interest, and takes in all the points you wish to put across.

Here are a few suggestions to help you gain and hold the interest of your audience.

Tell it like a story. Presenting your ideas in the same way that you would tell a story to a friend is very effective in gaining the audience's undivided attention and trust. It involves a great deal of enthusiasm and a structured flow of events leading to the conclusion. People enjoy listening to a story whether it is about the new stationery or the annual operating plan. No matter how boring or complicated the content of the presentation, it becomes more interesting if you adopt this method of delivery.

Speak with a moderate speed. If you talk too quickly, you may lose the listener. On the other hand, if you are telling your story at a slow pace, you will bore them to death. Moderation is the best option – it keeps the audience interested and looking forward to hearing what is coming next.

I have to present in a foreign language. I have a strong accent and I'm worried I might make a fool of myself.

Avoid an artificial accent. Do not worry too much about your accent. If you have a regional accent, or you are presenting in a foreign language, trying to change the way you talk adds to the things you have to think about when presenting, which may confuse you. There is nothing wrong with having an accent which is different from the one your audience has. Instead of trying to change your accent, concentrate on speaking clearly and with a moderate speed, to make sure that everyone understands and can follow what you're saying.

 SELECTING THE RIGHT STYLE

There are two main presentation styles:

- formal
- informal.

Variations and combinations of both exist. Choose which to use according to the occasion.

I was asked to present at a conference, which I have never done before. Should I present in the same way I do with my colleagues?

In some situations, it is necessary to give a **formal talk** to a group of people. Occasions like sales meetings, public lectures, etc., require careful preparation and a formal style.

Again, there isn't one single right style for formal presentations. But there are some basic aspects of the presentation, to which personal variations can be added, and which can be used on different formal occasions.

- **Dressing appropriately.** It is important to be dressed formally and to the standard required by the occasion. A smart look could help boost your confidence, as well as the audience's confidence in you. This shows the audience that you respect them and have made the effort to dress appropriately.

- **Using the right language.** Using formal but simple language, with some funny remarks when appropriate, is one of the best ways to maintain your credibility and keep the audience interested. When faced with a formal situation, some people use over-elaborate and complicated words. Try to resist the temptation. You need to leave your audience with no room for misinterpretation.

- **Using cartoons or pictures on your slides.** Use your slides to tell some of the jokes. A formal slide is not necessarily one with words and complicated sentences. Funny sketches on your slides may be very effective in driving a point home, as well as entertaining the audience.

- **Introducing yourself and thanking the audience.** If there are people in the audience who don't know you, make sure you introduce yourself. You should also conclude by thanking everyone for being there and answering any questions if applicable.

Informal presentations range from a progress meeting with your project team, to a two-minute talk with your boss.

At such occasions most people in the audience know you. Some traditional presentation techniques – the ones we have drummed into our heads on training courses – may not apply to informal situations. For instance, there is no need to introduce yourself at the beginning to your immediate colleagues. You can afford to experiment with a few jokes as your colleagues are a friendlier audience. In such situations, remember the following:

- Address your audience as you would **normally** on a one-to-one basis.
- Be **brief** and **to the point** without getting too comfortable and forgetting about the time.
- the chances are that you know quite a lot about these people so use **examples** to which they can relate.
- Don't hesitate to make your presentation interactive if

you can. Turn it into a conversation and invite contributions.

● When appropriate, ask the experts in the audience to **confirm** your theories or assumptions. Use that to gain their support.

Occasionally your manager or a senior colleague will ask you the classic question: 'how are things going?' This is an opportunity for you to give a **one-minute presentation** without visual aids. This obviously requires a very informal style. However, be very brief, concise and to the point. If you feel that the boss is too busy and you need more time to explain your point, book a slot with him or her to discuss matters further.

③ USING EFFECTIVE BODY LANGUAGE

When you look at people in the street, it is amazing how much you can tell about them by simply observing their **body language**.

Usually people form an impression about you within the first five minutes of meeting face-to-face. When presenting an hour is, in most cases, the maximum time you have to keep or change that impression.

Your body language has a lot to do with that impression. People described as 'charismatic' are those who are liked for no apparent reason. These people tend to be noticed as they enter a room. This is mainly achieved by the way they do and say things.

When presenting, your body language should reflect a confident, truthful and trustworthy personality, with a good sense of humour. It helps you convince people more. Following are some indicators on how to use your body language effectively.

Using your hands

- Use your hands to invite the audience to accept your point by having your palms upwards.

- Keep your palms open and your fingers together when moving your hands, release your fingers into a natural position if your hand is simply hanging on the side.

- Avoid closing your hand firmly as this can be interpreted as aggressive.

- Avoid rubbing your hands as this is a sign of nervousness.

- Use a pointer to keep one of your hands busy, but don't fiddle with it.

- Pointing with one finger at the audience can be interpreted as a warning sign. If this is not the intention, avoid doing it.

- Co-ordinate your hand movements with your words.

Using facial expressions and eye contact

- Use your eyebrows to articulate your feelings. When they point up, like when asking a question, you are inviting people to accept your suggestion. When frowning, coupled with the appropriate hand movement, you help people focus on a point with you.

- Move your head around and look people in the eye. Do not focus on one person only.

- Look at people even if they are not looking at you. People tend to look at your visual aids projected behind you for most of the time. Sometimes they might take their eyes off them and expect to see you talking to them and not looking at the piece of paper in front of you.

Controlling your movement

- Restrict your movements to the necessary ones. Some nervous presenters tend to take a few steps back every time they look up at the audience, then move forward when they look at their notes or the overhead projector (OHP).

- Face the audience, not the board behind you. If you are using any kind of projection equipment, especially an OHP, it is very important not to keep looking back at the projected image. This makes you look nervous and irritates the audience.

 TAKING CONTROL

By applying the techniques discussed earlier in this chapter, you leave little reason for the audience to be irritated or annoyed. Now take a further step and try to **keep them interested in your presentation** without giving you trouble. To do that, they must feel relaxed and on top of what is being said. If you are **in control**, you can achieve that easily.

It is more about controlling yourself than the audience. Once you are in full control of your actions and nerves, you can feel more comfortable in interacting with your audience. The following points will help you achieve that.

- **Show your interest** in the subject. If you're not interested why should they be?

- **Define the structure** of your presentation, and don't deviate too much and too often.
- **Involve the audience** by asking specific questions and guiding them to the answers shortly afterwards.
- **Be confident.**

One of the best ways to feel confident and less nervous is to practise. Practice boosts your confidence and helps you stay in control.

Like a sports game, the more time and effort you spend practising, the better you become.

Tips on how you can rehearse effectively

- Choose a topic that you feel passionately about and prepare a five-minute presentation on it.
- Stand in front of a mirror and present to yourself.
- Repeat this several times, each time observing a different aspect of your style.
- Repeat this several times, each time observing a different aspect of your style.
- Try to change any habits which contradict the rules of the game described in this chapter.
- Experiment with the various techniques and find out which ones suit the occasion you are pretending to be in.
- Try to film yourself with a video camera if one is available.
- Replay the film and observe yourself. This will help you find your mistakes and correct them.
- Get a friend to watch you and give you constructive criticism.
- Do not give up easily, it takes time to change old habits.

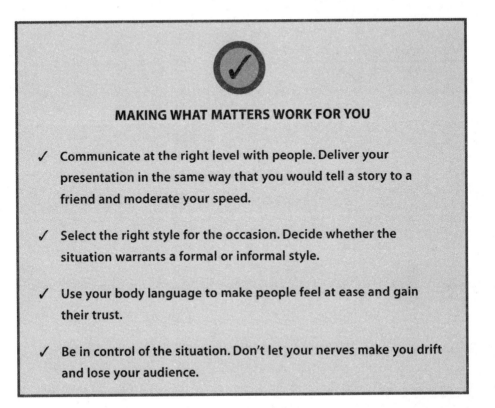

MAKING WHAT MATTERS WORK FOR YOU

✓ Communicate at the right level with people. Deliver your presentation in the same way that you would tell a story to a friend and moderate your speed.

✓ Select the right style for the occasion. Decide whether the situation warrants a formal or informal style.

✓ Use your body language to make people feel at ease and gain their trust.

✓ Be in control of the situation. Don't let your nerves make you drift and lose your audience.

2 Preparing the Presentation Material

Failing to prepare is preparing to fail.

4

things that
really matter

1 **RESEARCHING THE SUBJECT**

2 **SELECTING THE CONTENT**

3 **KEEPING IT TO THE POINT**

4 **WRITING A SCRIPT**

Before launching into a presentation, always consider carefully what should be said and to what level of detail. Remember that presenting is about **turning information into a simple and concise message**. Taking the time to prepare and think carefully about what needs to be said always pays off. Many people are increasingly finding that they have to present on subjects with which they are not familiar. This means that they will need to gain a certain amount of knowledge in a short time.

The other situation is when people are presented with the opportunity to present on a subject they know a great deal about. The tendency then is to cram as much information as possible into the presentation. This often results in an **information overload** for the audience, which confuses everyone.

IS THIS YOU?

● *I've been asked to give a presentation on a project where at least 20 people are involved. How am I going to get their input before the end of next week?* ● *I gave a one-hour presentation at a conference last month. My department wants me to present it to them in a five-minute slot next week.* ● *I have just started a new job and my predecessor was supposed to present at a conference in two weeks time. Unfortunately, he hasn't left me anything to present.* ● *No one in our department except me understands this technology. I've been asked to prepare a ten-minute presentation explaining it in simple terms.*

① RESEARCHING THE SUBJECT

Whether you are an expert in the subject or know little about it, you need to do some **research** to come up with the **right material for your presentation**. Research becomes more important when you do not know much about the subject, or when your presentation requires up-to-date statistics and figures or, possibly, input from other people.

Throughout your research activities, keep reminding yourself of the **objectives** of your presentation and the **audience** you are presenting to. This helps to focus on the **right type** and **depth** of information. Researching involves several steps which, if not carefully followed, may result in an ill-prepared presentation.

Before embarking on the research task, ask the following **basic questions**:

- **How much** do I already know about the subject?
- **Who** am I presenting to?

- For **how long** am I presenting?
- **When** and in **what setting** is the presentation taking place?

These questions will help you determine the scope of the work.

Gathering **background information** may require you to think differently on different occasions. For instance, reading a report or paper requires a different thought process from interviewing someone. If your research takes you to different parts of the country, careful planning saves you travel time.

Gathering information is not easy, so put considerable effort into it. The **more effort** you put in at this stage, the **fewer problems** you will face later.

To **identify sources of information**, treat your research as a small project. Start by identifying the **topics** you need to cover and work out ways of getting the relevant materials. Find out about the **location** of each piece of the 'puzzle'. When you know where to find what you need, check if it is feasible in the given time. If not, cut down on the activities and find alternatives. Check that you can actually get to the information you need when you plan to obtain it. For example, call the library to find out if the information you need is fully or partially held there and where else you can find it.

You are asked to prepare a presentation on the quality of education in your area. Write down five sources of information which could assist you in putting such a presentation together. Then write a plan on how and when it is feasible to obtain that information. You have one week.

You need to **manage your time** carefully.

- Find out how much **time** you have.
- Work out a **schedule** and try to stick to it.
- Divide the work into **small, measurable tasks** so that you can keep tight control over your timetable.
- Draw up a **plan of action** where you correlate the task with its geographical location and the time of day. Also check opening times of libraries and availability of people before you finalise your plan.
- List all activities clearly in a **timetable** with the date and estimated time for completion. Make sure you leave some buffer time in case things don't go to schedule.
- Leave an **empty column** on your table and place a tick next to each accomplished task.
- List any **alternative actions** to take should the original plan fail.
- Keep the **information** on the plan to a minimum. Refer to another document if there is a need to put in more details.

You don't always have to make transcripts of interviews with people. You can ask their permission to tape the conversation, and make brief notes related to the points of interest. This can help you focus on the important part of the interview later on.

Storing data:

- File the information and index the files.
- If you have access to a computer database, save the information there and create easy-to-follow search fields. However, a database does not have to be computerised and can be held in a filing system or ring-binder.

- Some records can't be kept in the same format as the others, e.g. audio tapes of interviews, videos, news cuttings, etc. Keep these under the appropriate indexing system and refer to them in your database.

 SELECTING THE CONTENT

Once you have gathered the information, **put it into words** and **filter out what is not essential** for the talk. Any information which you gather, but don't include in your presentation, can be useful when answering questions.

Make life easier and don't start with trying to write the introduction. Leave that until after you have decided on the content of the presentation. The introduction then writes itself.

After gathering the information you become more familiar with the subject you are going to present and ideas start coming to your mind. Use a **brainstorming** session to write all these ideas on paper. During this session apply the following process:

- Write down the headings of the topics at random on the paper.
- When you run out of topics, go back to your research notes to see if you can find some more.
- On a new sheet of paper, group the ideas under separate headings.
- If you can't find a suitable place for an idea, leave it aside for a while. You may fit it in the right place later.

Don't aim for perfection because you may never be satisfied with any results. This may lead you to spend longer than anticipated and run out of precious time for the activities that follow. However, this should not be an excuse for a poor presentation. Make sure you have some extra time in your schedule for last-minute changes, because you might get a new idea after you've written your script and want to move things about.

 KEEPING IT TO THE POINT

Time is a key factor which determines what you can include in your presentation. After having spent a lot of time and effort collecting information, you may feel compelled to use it all in your presentation.

One of the major contributors to the nervous states in which presenters often find themselves is running over the allocated time. The questions you ask yourself at the beginning of research should help you to avoid this situation.

If you know too much about the subject, or you have done extensive research, you may have a lot to share with your audience with very little time to do so.

To avoid over-running and still deliver an effective message, keep your presentation to the point. To do that, **classify the information** you have gathered and apply some filtering. Classify the topics and points under three headings:

- **Essential** (has to be included in the presentation at any cost).
- **Helpful** (helps to clarify the message but can be cut down).

- **Nice to have** (supporting material which can be the first to be filtered out).

Once you have classified your content under these three categories, it is possible to remove the parts that are not essential or helpful in putting your message across. The same technique can be used after you have written the second draft of your script and timed yourself reading it (see next section).

 WRITING A SCRIPT

It is useful to have a **script**, even if you are not going to read it word for word. The **more comfortable** you are with the subject, the **less words** you need on your script. If you are very confident about your knowledge, your script may be reduced to a short outline.

Script writing is a three-stage process.

1. Preparing the first draft.
2. Putting the second draft together.
3. Attending to the grammar and use of effective language.

When preparing the **first draft**:

- Start developing your ideas into a short story.
- Rely on your memory to start with to see what you can put together without referring to your notes. This helps you clarify your ideas and find out how much you know about the subject.
- Refer to your notes when you get stuck.
- Try to find any points that you failed to recollect.

- Do not, at this stage, worry about your writing style or grammar as this will delay your thinking process.

The second draft requires a slightly more detailed approach. Look at the structure of the script and make sure that the transition between sections or topics flows smoothly. If two consecutive ideas are not related, the shift between them becomes noticeable and the presentation loses its continuity and flow. Find a link or a point in common with both ideas and insert it between them.

- Put all sections in the right order to facilitate smooth transition between them.
- Add the right sentences at the beginning and end of each section for a smooth transition.
- Read the script out loud to get a feel of what it sounds like.

After checking the transitions, it is time to divert your attention towards the **grammar** and **use of language**. This is the fine-tuning stage.

- A safe option is to make the tone slightly on the formal side without making the talk sound dull. In general, it is more appropriate to use the third person – they, he, hers. However, do not hesitate to use the first person – I, we – when appropriate. Try not to get carried away with the use of the first person, but do not avoid it altogether.
- Avoid expressing yourself in a negative way and use positive terms whenever you can. 'Challenges' or 'opportunities' are better than 'problems'.
- Using factual language reflects a friendly and convincing

tone. Extravagant expressions can only help confuse the listener.

- Read your script carefully. Read it again.

- Make any changes that you think can place more emphasis on certain points.

- As you read, start to imagine what diagrams, pictures or charts can be used to help you explain your points.

- If there is an idea that cannot be supported by visual elements, make it shorter and include it with a closely related one.

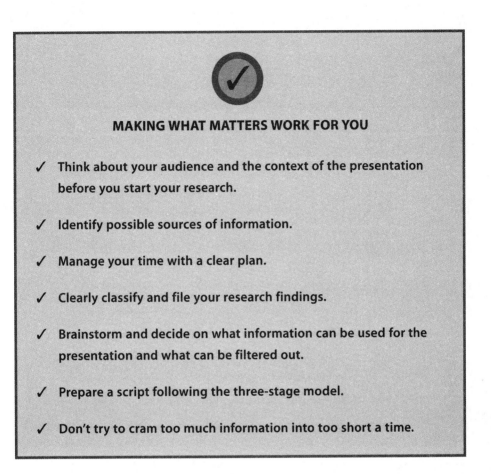

MAKING WHAT MATTERS WORK FOR YOU

✓ Think about your audience and the context of the presentation before you start your research.

✓ Identify possible sources of information.

✓ Manage your time with a clear plan.

✓ Clearly classify and file your research findings.

✓ Brainstorm and decide on what information can be used for the presentation and what can be filtered out.

✓ Prepare a script following the three-stage model.

✓ Don't try to cram too much information into too short a time.

3 Planning Your Talk

Time is short.
Planning helps you make you make effective use of it.

4 things that really matter

1 **DRAWING A PRESENTATION LAYOUT**
2 **KNOWING WHAT TO SAY AND WHEN TO SAY IT**
3 **AIMING TO SELL AN IDEA, NOT TO FILL TIME**
4 **BACKING UP YOUR MEMORY**

To get your message across effectively, make efficient use of the given time to **address the key issues**. A well planned presentation is a well received one. **Keep it clear** and avoid too much crammed information. By investing some time in **planning and designing** the content of your presentation, you can become more confident about your delivery.

Use the time to put your imagination to the test and see what it can come up with. Group your words under separate **frames**. No matter what kind of visual materials and aids you use, you have to create frames within which you put your ideas and sentences.

Spending time combining what goes on your slides with what you say gives your presentation a professional feel, which helps you in putting your point across.

Stay focussed on the objective of the presentation. This helps you in filtering out irrelevant information and in remembering the key points you need to cover.

IS THIS YOU?

● *Time seems to go very fast when I present and I seldom manage to cover all the topics I intend to highlight.* ● *My mind goes blank and I find it very hard to pick the right words at the right time when I am presenting.* ● *I feel very nervous, especially when I don't have enough time to cover everything.* ● *Everyone else seems to run over time and I always end up with less time than originally allocated.*

DRAWING A PRESENTATION LAYOUT

A good presentation is mainly driven by what is on the slides. The rule of thumb is that **if it is significant, it should definitely be included on the slide**. Throughout this book, the term 'slides' is used to refer to any frame within which visual aid materials are presented, including computer presentations, 35 mm slides, transparencies etc.

You can arrange your ideas in several ways, depending on the reaction that you expect from your audience.

To ensure the right flow of information, take the following three-step approach:

● **Hostile audience:** start with the least controversial statement, gradually putting forward arguments and reasons for your suggestions. Conclude with your proposal.

● **Friendly audience:** start by stating the main point, then move on to explain why you are proposing this idea not another.

● **Indifferent audience:** this is particularly the case when you are presenting on the progress of a project or any subject where there is no one right answer. Take your audience through a journey in a story-telling style.

A general rule for deciding on how many slides to use in a given time is to allocate about 5 to 10% of the total presentation time on each slide or about two minutes, whichever is shorter.

When considering the **content of your slides**:

- Put the least possible information on your slides and keep it to the point.

- The content of the slides should be directly related to what you are saying. Don't let your talk drift away from the immediate content of the slide that is showing.

- Include on your slides what your audience will be expecting. Some audiences prefer more pictures than words, other prefer the opposite. If in doubt, use a balance of illustrations and words without overdoing it either way.

- Make use of flow charts and diagrams to illustrate complicated ideas, especially in technical presentations.

- Consider alternative ways of presenting charts. For example, a chart on population growth could be built out of match-stick people rather than simple bars.

- Do not photocopy pages from books or reports. Always produce illustrations with a consistent style throughout the presentation.

- Produce clear and concise slides prepared to a good standard. Try to make use of computer packages to help you prepare the content to a professional standard. Alternatively, hand-drawn diagrams are acceptable if the occasion is less formal.

If you are **combining text with slides**, treat your presentation like a screen play or a short film, using a

storyboard or a **treatment** to link the script to the picture.
A treatment is a document where you divide your script into
small sections and write them one under the other, perhaps
in a tabulated form. You then write a description of the

Treatment

Text	*Slide contents*
.... It is essential for you to update your skills to join the wave of change and keep up with the changes in things surrounding us.	Man surfing and reading a book Title: Keeping up with the changes
....Computers are becoming an essential tool in modern communications and in every-day life. Struggling with them will be a constant struggle with modern life.	Man fighting computer Title: Struggling with modern life

---

... It is essential for you to update your skills to join the wave of change and keep up with the changes in things surrounding us.

Keeping up with the changes

... Computers are becoming an essential tool in modern communications and in everyday life. Struggling with them will be a constant struggle with modern life.

Struggling with modern life

related slide next to each section. If you are good at sketching, you can sketch the content of the slide instead of just having a description. This then becomes a storyboard.

 ## KNOWING WHAT TO SAY AND WHEN TO SAY IT

You have now looked at how to structure your presentation and use the appropriate style for different occasions. Having covered the basics it is time to move to the next level and consider some more professional techniques which can enhance your talk further.

If you are completely unknown to the audience, start by **introducing yourself** and what you do, to establish the level of authority with which you speak on the subject. However, if you have been introduced by someone else, all you need to do is thank the person who introduced you and, if appropriate, the body or organisation that invited you to speak.

Follow the same principle as with the content of your slides for the three expected audience reactions: hostile, friendly and indifferent. In addition you can:

- Start by immediately involving the audience through **questions** that will make them think about the subject. An example would be: 'Have you ever worked out how many hours your employees spend travelling to and from the office and how many good ideas they generate when they are outside the normal office environment?' This could be a good introduction for a talk on tele-working.

- Start with an **unexpected statement** to seize the audience's attention. 'The Internet is a platform for pornography to thrive on … That's what the cynics say.'

Memorise the opening lines because this helps you get over your nervousness and get into the talk comfortably.

Next start to plan the **body** of your presentation:

- Start by highlighting the **overall content** of your presentation.
- Throughout the presentation insert **summaries** and **reminders** of what was covered and what is still to be covered.
- Insert **funny remarks** and **light-hearted comparisons** in your presentation, especially if the subject is dry.
- Ask **direct questions** every now and then. As you do that, look at those who you think are drifting away. You can then provide the answer without embarrassing anyone by really expecting them to respond.

People can only fully concentrate for the first 10 to 15 minutes of a presentation, if your lucky. If you want them to stay with you mentally, you need to keep them interested.

Your **closing statement** in the presentation should be memorable. After summarising what the talk was all about, a final reminder of the single point that describes your talk is in order. This helps the audience to leave the room with at least one thought in their mind, which could trigger a recollection of the presentation's contents.

Think hard about your final words and try to memorise them at the planning stage. **The conclusion is as important as the beginning**. Don't be afraid to be a bit dramatic or poetic in your ending, as long as it is still to the point. If appropriate, you can let the audience know that you will be taking questions, but always make sure that the last few words are to thank the audience for listening.

 AIMING TO SELL AN IDEA, NOT TO FILL TIME

As you plan your talk, you can insert some **rhetorical tricks** to make your talk more effective in selling an idea. At first, these need to be inserted consciously. However, with experience they will come naturally to you.

These tricks are widely used in public speaking. Listen to good political speeches at party conferences and you will notice that they are full of them. The most common ones are:

- **contrast**
- **repetition**
- **lists of three.**

Here is an example of how all three tricks can be combined in one paragraph selling the idea of setting up a local community youth centre with a specially arranged fund:

1. If you think that not having a community centre contributes to the increase in youth crime – this is the solution …
2. If you think providing a centre for the community is financially impossible – this is the solution …
3. And if you think a youth centre will make our community a better place to live in – then support our centre because it will …

Notice the contrast in lines 1 and 2 with the statement of the problem and the solution. 'If you think – this is' are the repetitions in the paragraph which re-emphasise the thinking process. The paragraph is also made of a list of three which builds up to a spectacular ending. This paragraph is only for illustration, but these tricks can be used separately.

A dramatic delivery with the right pauses can earn applause in public speeches and approval in smaller or professional presentations.

Work on finding the right wording:

- Avoid the use of unnecessary words or phrases like 'more or less', 'that's a very good question', etc.
- Make a conscious effort not to use time-filling words like 'em' and 'er'. Silence can be used to give people time to think.
- Explain any acronyms.
- Avoid being patronising by imposing your ideas and expecting people to immediately accept them.

Make effective use of the time available for your presentation. Throughout your preparations, be conscious of the amount of time you have to speak for. When your presentation is ready, rehearse it and time yourself. Don't time the speed at which you read from a script because you normally talk more slowly than when you read. Some people prefer to roughly memorise the words from their speech and find it helps them to finish on time. However, this could be a problem if things change on the day and you are asked to shorten your presentation.

Learn to have a feel for the timing when you present. This comes with practice. It can be helped by comparing the time it takes you to read a certain paragraph with explaining to someone, in similar words, what this paragraph was all about.

Remember to include in your time allocation the time it will take you to get up and prepare yourself to start and also the time it takes to switch from one slide to the other.

You are required to tell the truth and nothing but the truth, but not necessarily the whole truth as this may take too long. Leave that for the question time.

 BACKING UP YOUR MEMORY

There are three main ways of delivering a talk:

- **Memorising the content.**
- **Reading from a script.**
- **Using notes.**

Memorising the content is the most natural and effective way. Once you have written or outlined a script, you can memorise the key points you want to mention and rehearse a few times to become comfortable with the delivery. You do not have to recite the script word for word, so your talk sounds more natural and sincere.

Reading from a script is the safest but most formal option. However, there is a risk of appearing insincere. If you don't have time to memorise and rehearse a script, this could be a good option to avoid missing any points. Should you decide to do that, be conscious of the fact that reading from a script is not an excuse to ignore the delivery techniques such as **pauses, articulation, volume, emphasis**, etc. There is no reason why you can't make it sound natural when you read from a script. Avoid the temptation of letting the script act as a barrier between you and your audience.

If you know your subject reasonably well, but are not confident enough to remember everything, using notes can help. If you decide to use notes, use the following general rules:

- Include only the main points, not the entire script.

- Use small, stiff note cards for easy handling.

- Keep them short and to the minimum.

- Keep important facts on a separate note in case you are asked for more details later.

If you know your subject well, your slides could act as triggers for expanding on certain points. Only use this method when you can actually see the slides without having to look back at the projection behind you.

MAKING WHAT MATTERS WORK FOR YOU

✓ Sequence your ideas in a clear way that addresses the key issues.

✓ Co-ordinate your slides with your script just like they do in film-making.

✓ Tailor your introduction and conclusion to your audience and memorise them.

✓ Choose your closing words carefully as you want your audience to remember them.

✓ Make effective use of rhetorical tricks.

✓ Rehearse your presentation several times to make sure it fits your allocated slot. Leave some extra time for unexpected delays.

✓ Decide on which memory backup method you want to use long before the presentation and give yourself time to rehearse with it.

4 Presenting with Visual Aids

Seeing is believing.
With presentations, seeing is understanding.

Visual aids offer your audience a visual representation of your thoughts. They help you to drive a point home more effectively. It is easier to express yourself with the use of **pictures, graphs** and **models**. Think how hard it is to describe the design of a building, for example. No matter how articulate you are, the person you are describing it to will never be able to re-construct the same picture in their imagination. It may be close, but not the same. You can try this experiment and see how much fun you have, with little result.

Visual aids also play the role of **keeping the audience interested** in the presentation as well as helping you to **deliver an effective message**.

Two-thirds of what is stored in our memory comes through the eyes. So if you want people to remember more of what you tell them, you need to show it to them.

IS THIS YOU?

● I always use slides when I present but people still don't seem to understand what I'm talking about ● I have always given speeches without visual aids and they seem to go down well with the audience. Unfortunately they don't seem to remember much of them later. ● I've been asked to give a technical presentation next week to a group of non-technical people. I don't know how to explain complicated designs to them. ● My computer gives me the capability to produce very nice pictures and animations, but I never seem to get the right colour combinations when I print my slides.

① USING PICTURES TO DELIVER YOUR MESSAGE

Imagine road warning signs without pictures. How long would it take you to read 'warning, dangerous slippery road'? Long enough for you to have an accident.

Taking road signs as an example, colour and simple messages tell us something in a very short time. The same principle should be adopted for making presentation slides.

A clear slide consists of a **heading** and **body**. The heading is usually written in larger font and describes, in brief, what is presented in the slide. The body is reserved for the material you want to present. In the body you may combine pictures, diagrams and words. To create effective content, remember the following rules:

- **KIS** (Keep It Simple).

- **Use pictures or diagrams** whenever you can and keep the number of words and figures to a minimum.

- **Leave plenty of space** between items for visibility.

- **Use large fonts** for better visibility. Generally, the font size for body text should not be less than 14.

- Your drawings do not have to be perfect, but take care in making them **clear and meaningful**.

- **Keep the same general appearance** throughout your presentation, using the same background colour, font type, etc. Only break consistency if you want to use this as a shock element.

② ADDING COLOUR FOR GREATER IMPACT

There is nothing wrong with black and white presentations, especially when various levels of grey shading can be used. However, colour can be used to add an extra dimension to the media you are using for explaining a point. Black and white road signs are helpful, but it is easier to spot a danger sign with red around it.

Colour is a powerful way to make important information stand out, adding a professional finish to a presentation.

Colour is the reflected light wave length that varies in different materials. Different colours can be created by combining two or more **base colours**. If two colours are placed next to each other they can create the illusion of a **third colour** when viewed from a distance.

Six main colours can be identified, excluding black and white. They are all related to one another. By varying the darkness of one colour you can gradually move to the next one. Using this relationship, you can place them in a circle, often referred to as the 'colour wheel'. For example, orange is a darker form of yellow and a lighter form of red. Between any two colours, there is a large number of hues. From this relationship, it is possible to identify which two colours go well together.

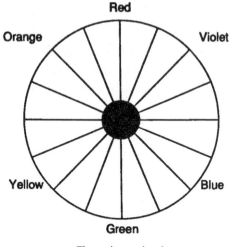

The colour wheel.

Colours can be combined for effective use. If two opposing colours like red and green are put next to each other, they cause a 'vibration' effect and make the viewer uncomfortable. However, if you choose to use this combination, you can vary the darkness and brightness of each colour to achieve harmony.

In order to combine colours for better impact and harmony, remember the following:

- To achieve **harmony**, two hues next to each other on the colour wheel can be used.

- To create a **contrast** between two ideas, or make a point stand out from the background colour, select two hues with three colours between them on the colour wheel.

- black and white are also two important colours that should not be completely ignored. Planning the use of black and white should be part of your strategy to use colour.

Black writing is good on yellow backgrounds and white works well with a dark blue background.

- Use colour consistently with accepted conventions. Red, for example, can be used to indicate warning while green is connected to safety. It does not make sense if you show company losses in green.

- Don't use colour simply to decorate your slide. It is there to add value.

- Use colour to show the relationships between two items. For example, in charts colour can be used as an extra axis.

- Space coloured objects out and allow enough space for the colour to be visible.

- Use bright colours on dark backgrounds for greater effect.

 WORKING WITH COMPUTERS

Most professional presentations today are created using a computer. There are many **computer programmes** that could help you create slide layouts, colour schemes, pictures, graphs, etc. However, what you see on your computer screen may look different when printed on transparency. You can use **scanners** to scan photographs, pictures or designs into your computer, enhance them if necessary and use them as part of your presentation. The **Internet** is also a good source of clipart and photographs.

When using Internet sources, always make sure they are either available for the public to use or you obtain the necessary permission to use them. The fact that a picture is on the Internet does not necessarily mean it is not protected by copyright.

On-screen presentations are being used increasingly. They are the most environmentally friendly as they do not require any printing. All you need is a special **data projector** which can be connected to your computer. Slides can then be projected directly from the package you used to create them. This also allows you to introduce **multi-media presentations**, provided your computer and projector support that facility. **Sound** and **video clips** can be added to the same presentation without the need of additional equipment. Some advanced presentation packages also allow you to introduce **animations** to your presentation. All this can be confusing to both you and your audience. To avoid confusion, remember the following:

- Animations can help you build your slides with great effect, but don't over-use them.

- Check the speed of slide transitions and animations with the equipment you intend to use as sometimes they might be slower when viewed on your computer screen alone.

- Try to avoid random transitions and incorporate ones which follow on from the previous slide.

- Build slides gradually. Various sections of the slide can be added gradually at the click of the mouse button. This gives you time to explain your ideas point by point without the audience jumping ahead of you by reading the next line.

- Refer to equipment and software manuals for information on how to use them effectively.

④ **CHOOSING THE RIGHT EQUIPMENT**
The choice of equipment and other visual aid media is

changing with time. The general choice available is listed in the table below, with advantages and disadvantages.

Method	Advantage	Disadvantage
Overhead projector (OHP)	• Widely available • Allows you to see your slide • You can point without having to turn towards the screen	• Bulky • Requires the production of transparencies (which need reprinting when changes happen)
Slide projector	• Good picture quality • Professional look and feel	• Only works in dark rooms • Irritating transitions through black
Data projector	• Saves printing • Allows animations and integrated multi-media • Professional look and feel	• Not widely available • May require a dark room • May not work with your computer • Checking required and adapters may be needed

Other media can be used in addition such as **flip charts** or **videos**, to illustrate certain points or help explain some concepts. Avoid the use of purely promotional videos that do not add any real value to your presentations. People can see right through them, which may lose you some credibility.

There are five aspects to consider when making a decision on what technology or media to use.

1. the ability to grab the audience's attention.

2. The size of the equipment and practicality of use.

3. The suitability of the equipment for the occasion – for

example a data projector may not be suitable for a small informal presentation where transparencies can suffice.

4. The effect on the audience – consider if it will add any value.

5. Convenience and availability – make sure that the equipment you require is available at the venue.

Sometimes the most impressive technology may fail at the last minute. Make sure you always have an alternative method as backup.

 ## USING NOTES AND HANDOUTS

Notes and **handouts** can also act as visual aids. They can help you explain your points if used effectively. It is also sometimes useful to provide the audience with something they can refer to during or after the presentation in case they miss a certain point. Effective handouts would include a scaled down version of a slide accompanied by more detailed notes underneath. Try to provide handouts only when needed and avoid giving them out at the beginning of the presentation if you can help it. This is particularly important if you are trying to use an element of surprise.

Handouts can be produced using the same computer package as the presentation and automatically built from the original slides. Diagrams, the details of which may be forgotten when the corresponding transparency is removed, can be included in your handouts for the audience to refer to.

Notes can also be distributed after the presentation for the audience to refer to. These should include details and figures which may or may not have been mentioned in the presentation. They should also be planned carefully and produced in the form of a short report.

MAKING WHAT MATTERS WORK FOR YOU

✓ Reduce the amount of information per slide to the minimum.

✓ Visual aids are there to help you, not to make your life more complicated, so keep it simple.

✓ Use colour for additional impact.

✓ Learn which colour combinations achieve harmony and which create effective contrasts.

✓ Choose the right type of visual aids for the occasion. There is no such thing as one ideal visual aid.

✓ Make sure you are familiar with the visual aid equipment and you are comfortable using it.

✓ Careful use of notes and handouts will increase the effectiveness of your presentation. It gives people something to refer to.

5 Speaking Effectively

Speaking is less about what you say than how you say it.

4

things that
really matter

1 **DEVELOPING AN INTERESTING VOICE**
2 **USING SILENCE AND PAUSES EFFECTIVELY**
3 **USING STRESS AND EMPHASIS**
4 **PROJECTING YOUR VOICE**

Experience has shown that **what you say** accounts for about 7% of the overall effect of a presentation, while about 40% is accounted for by **the way you say it**. Your voice, together with your body language, are the second most important contributors to the success of your presentation after visual aids.

For an effective presentation most, if not not all, of the audience's senses should be involved:

- they **see** you and what's on the slides
- they can **participate** in a demonstration by touching or smelling something
- they **listen** to you.

Voice is a powerful tool when used effectively in a presentation or a speech. Think about great speakers, those who left an impact on your life, and think about their voices and the way they controlled them.

IS THIS YOU?

● I can't raise my voice enough for people in a large auditorium to hear me. ● I feel compelled to fill the silence when I present so I find myself talking fast and hardly pausing for a breath. ● I prepare very good visual aids but I don't seem to be able to capture the attention of my audience for a long time. ● Some speakers are so natural. I tend to sound very artificial when I present.

① DEVELOPING AN INTERESTING VOICE

It is possible to identify and improve on four characteristics of your speech: **tone, pitch, volume** and **clarity**. You may be good at some and need improvement at others. This section will help you improve in all of these areas.

If you hit an empty glass with a fork it produces a different **tone** from when it is full or half-full. Your voice works in the same way. If you constrict your body cavities which are responsible for amplifying sound, your voice will sound restricted and sometimes nasal. Restricting body cavities can happen by standing or sitting in the wrong way. Make sure **all your limbs are relaxed** and that you **stand in a natural, upright position**. Avoid arching your back forwards or backwards.

Your vocal chords are like guitar strings. When stretched they produce a different **pitch** from when they are loosened. When stretched, the number of vibrations your vocal chords produce increases due to the short distance allowed for them to vibrate. These vibrations produce a high-pitched sound. The opposite happens when the vocal chords are loosened up. This produces a **lower pitch** or a **deeper, warmer voice**.

The **volume** of your voice can be increased in two different ways. the first is by increasing the pressure of air coming out of your lungs. The second is by narrowing the space between the vocal chords (glottis). You can increase the volume of a whisper by increasing the **pressure of air** flowing through your glottis.

Clarity is determined by the speech organs and how well you can control them. If you are too nervous your tongue and lips start playing tricks on you because they are tense. In order to make sure that you are understood, remember the following:

- **Exercise your speech organs** by consciously controlling every move on your tongue. If you find this difficult when speaking fast, slow down. The conscious effort becomes second nature after a while.

- Make an effort to **move your lips**. This helps the listener to work out what you are saying too, even if they can't hear you very well.

- If you are presenting in a foreign language, it is important to **pronounce clearly** and **speak more slowly** than normal.

Finding the **right pitch** is also important. People generally feel more comfortable listening to a smooth, deep voice than a high-pitched one. However, sometimes they feel comfortable enough to go to sleep. So don't try to force the pitch of your voice lower than its normal limits as this will not only make it sound artificial, but it will make you lose your voice too. Some speakers tend to stretch their voices higher than their natural pitch, because of nervous tension, especially at the beginning of a presentation.

The most natural way of speaking is to identify your natural pitch and use it, together with slight variation to add vitality to your talk.

To find your natural pitch, do the following:

1. Speak at the lowest note that feels comfortable to you.

2. Use a musical instrument and find the note which corresponds to your lowest comfortable pitch.

3. Move four notes up the musical scale. The fourth note should be very close to your natural pitch.

4. Try to tune your voice with this note and speak with the music for a while to help you get used to that tune.

5. Practise this as many times as you need to become confident in finding your natural pitch very quickly.

 USING SILENCE AND PAUSES EFFECTIVELY

Sometimes, **silence** can be more effective than words. Many presenters feel compelled to fill the silence because they are too scared of it. They end up using sounds such as 'emm' and 'er'.

A short pause may feel like a long time to the speaker but to the audience it is a chance to absorb the information, or wake up if they are falling asleep.

Pauses can help you relax and breathe. They can also help you put your thoughts together to start elaborating on a new idea. Here are some useful hints on the uses of pauses:

- Don't feel compelled to fill the silence. If you are enthusiastic about the subject and find yourself speaking quickly, force yourself to pause. Use your body language to show the enthusiasm, not the speed of your speech.

- Moderate the speed of your talk to the level of its contents.

- Try to maintain the rhythm and the rate of flow of ideas throughout your presentation.

The aim is to be understood, not to say as many words as possible within a given time or to fill the whole time with words.

③ USING STRESS AND EMPHASIS

Pauses are not the only way to **emphasise a point**. The amount of stress put on a syllable can also have a good effect. Avoid over-using emphasis. This diminishes the effect of this technique and renders it useless. Think about the message you are trying to put across and plan your emphasis accordingly. There are many ways of using emphasis in speech.

One way is to **vary the pitch**, going up and then down at the end of the word or series of words, e.g. 'the design was based on the *latest technology available*.' Say 'latest' with a high pitch and go down to reach your natural pitch at 'available'. This makes the series of words sound more important than the rest of the sentence. Words can also be emphasised by putting some energy in them and saying them decisively, e.g. 'this is the *only way* to do it.'

Speaking decisively, with a decisive tone, is most effective with single words. However, in many cases emphasis is placed on a **group of words** rather than just one. The same technique applies as for single words, but with a group of words the decisive tone can be extended to include all the words in the group.

Use pauses and emphases effectively by spreading them throughout your presentation.

A pause right after an emphasis can have a double effect. Try to emphasise through pitch change more often than by using a decisive tone, to avoid coming across as aggressive.

 PROJECTING YOUR VOICE

Actors can make you hear the quietest whisper from a distance. This proves that the voice can be projected without an increase in volume. **Voice projection** depends on two factors:

1. **Physical.**

2. **Psychological.**

The physical factor comprises:

- the force with which you breathe
- the muscular power you put into forming the words
- the clarity of your pronunciation.

As to the psychological factor, some people feel nervous in front of an audience and fail to project their voice sufficiently. In some cases, speakers over-compensate for their fear and project too much because they avoid looking at the audience.

In order to **estimate the projection power** required for a specific audience or room, look at the person furthest away from you and imagine you are talking to him or her. Psychologically you will feel the need to project your voice towards that person, and you will be able to **control your vocal organs and breathing** accordingly.

Use your body to help you project your voice, by increasing the resonance of your body cavities. To achieve maximum resonance, try the following:

- **Relax the muscles in your neck** and stand comfortably without bending or over-straightening your chest.

- Also relax the muscles in your neck by **nodding gently** a few times.
- **Take a deep breath and exhale**, letting out a deep sound. You can then feel how the cavity in your chest is working.
- If you have a cold, make sure you **clear your nose** before you start your presentation.
- **Relax your jaw** by totally relying on your hand to move your chin up and down a few times, without using the jaw muscles.
- **Relax your tongue** by stretching it out and letting it touch your lower teeth.

The upper part of your body has a major effect on projection and should be in a relaxed position for maximum resonance.

Your **posture** can add to that effect. Other cavities in the body can be used to create resonance and it helps if your posture is right. To achieve a good posture, try the following:

- Relax your shoulder muscles by raising and dropping them a few times.
- Do not bend forward as you speak. This prevents your chest cavity from resonating.
- Similarly, if you are standing with a curved back your voice projection will be restricted.

If your voice is shivering, this is usually due to nervous energy. Use your hands and body to channel that energy.

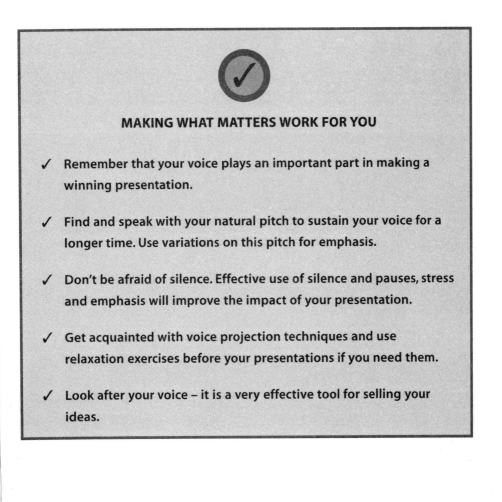

MAKING WHAT MATTERS WORK FOR YOU

✓ Remember that your voice plays an important part in making a winning presentation.

✓ Find and speak with your natural pitch to sustain your voice for a longer time. Use variations on this pitch for emphasis.

✓ Don't be afraid of silence. Effective use of silence and pauses, stress and emphasis will improve the impact of your presentation.

✓ Get acquainted with voice projection techniques and use relaxation exercises before your presentations if you need them.

✓ Look after your voice – it is a very effective tool for selling your ideas.

6 Managing Your Audience

Audience management is not about control but understanding.

As you feel confident with the basic presentation techniques, start thinking about the little extra things that could make your presentation even more effective. In a previous chapter, we have touched on the techniques used in preparing presentations for different types of audiences. This chapter will take a step further from that, by exploring **additional techniques** for presenting to **different audiences**.

In order to pitch your presentation at the right level you need to identify the type of audience you are addressing.

By knowing their 'hot buttons' and when to press them, you gain control of the situation.

Deal with a presentation as a group activity involving you and the people you are presenting to. Try to see yourself through their eyes. This will help you pitch it at the right level.

IS THIS YOU?

● *I never seem to pitch my presentation at the right level. It is either too technical or too simple.* ● *I present to multicultural audiences and I find it difficult to get the same reaction from everyone.* ● *When I present, I can't tell whether my message is getting across or not.* ● *I hear a lot about audience participation but I don't know how to do it naturally, without appearing too patronising.*

(1) SPEAKING THE AUDIENCE'S LANGUAGE

This does not necessarily mean speaking a foreign language. It refers to speaking in **a way that is understood** by your audience. For example, if your audience prefers simple, high-level presentations with diagrams and pictures, a technical presentation would not work. This sounds like common sense, but under pressure we are tempted to go with what is easier to us rather than with common sense.

There are different audience types, needing different types of address.

- **Experts** – you can get into technical details without having to explain the basics.

- **Different ages and backgrounds** – include brief explanations to those who are less likely to understand the technicalities. Let the experts know that you are doing this for the benefit of those who may not be familiar with the subject.

- **Non-experts** – this is very likely to happen in public lectures where the majority of the audience are not subject matter experts. Pitch your presentation at an appropriate level, without worrying too much about those who want details.

Regulate the speed of your presentation to the capacity of the audience to absorb its contents. If you notice your audience is getting impatient, it could be because you are spending too much time explaining a point.

Understanding the **cultural language** will help you make yourself understood. The cultural language again is not necessarily a foreign language but relates to the **conventions** accepted by different cultures. As the world is becoming a smaller place, we find ourselves increasingly dealing with people from other countries and, sometimes, other cultures. Some **jokes**, for example, may not be understood by people from other countries. **Pictures** may also mean different things to members of a multicultural audience. **Body language** is also important. In some countries, nodding your head means refusal or rejection. Try to find out about the cultural conventions of your audience beforehand. If you are presenting to a multicultural audience – this is particularly the case in international conferences – stay on the safe side and avoid making controversial statements. Use a more formal tone and a body language you feel comfortable with. You can start venturing out of these boundaries as you start detecting the reaction of your audience.

 KNOWING YOUR AUDIENCE

Before you try to convince your audience with an idea, it is useful to know what they want out of your presentation and how your proposed idea caters for their needs. Try to find as much as you can about your audience during the preparation stage. Some shorter presentations take place at exhibition stands to a total stranger who is passing by. By asking questions, try to judge the level of knowledge and interest of the person in front of you. Identify his or her

needs and reasons for wanting to know more, then tailor
your talk accordingly

You are **selling solutions**. Problems and challenges exist
everywhere. Think of your presentation as a way to provide
your audience with a solution to their problem or challenge,
be it current or in the future.

*People are more interested in what things can do for them than how
they do it. Your audience should always be the focal point of your
presentation.*

Here are some suggestions for selling ideas by selling
solutions:

- Identify the **problem** or the **challenge** as early as
  possible.
- Arouse the audience's **desire** by hitting the right chord.
  Focus on what is relevant.
- Desire may not be related to **need**. A customer may have
  the need for a certain product but the desire to have the
  latest version.
- Find out about the personal **thoughts** of the decision-
  makers. flatter them by referring to their expert
  knowledge if you can. This way you win them to your
  side.
- Position your **message** as a solution to their problem and
  a fulfilment of their desires.

③ READING THEIR BODY LANGUAGE

As you present, you can find out more about your audience.
Their body language tells you a great deal. It gives you the
chance to adjust your performance accordingly, by
changing the pace or stress, tone the humour up or down,

etc. Like reading a book, you can read your audience by looking at them as much as you can. Signs to spot:

- **Posture** – leaning forward is often a sign of interest or desire to be involved. You are very likely to get the first question from this person. Sometimes they get tired and sit back but this doesn't mean they have lost interest.

- **Arms and legs** – lack of interest is shown by forming barriers such as crossing arms or legs. Sometimes covering the face or mouth could be a sign of that too.

- **Eyes** – when people lose interest, their eyes start wandering outside the area where you are standing. Eyes can also tell whether a person is comfortable with what you are saying or showing them, or they are struggling to understand.

- **Clearing the throat** – people tend to do that when they lose interest. This could spread to the rest of the audience once the silence is broken.

- **Nodding** – this is a sign of acceptance. However, some people tend to nod continuously for no reason. After a while you can tell the difference between the two types.

④ AVOIDING CONFLICT AND ARGUMENT

It is common for presenters to be thought of as potential liars. You often hear remarks such as 'I'm not sure about these figures' or 'are you sure this is the best way to deal with this problem?' Such a **hostile environment** is not only created by the audience. It could be largely influenced by the presenter, by **handling escalations of conflict**.

Sometimes conflict can be triggered by a bad reaction to a negative action. This creates tension between the presenter and the audience, resulting in **failure to convince**. To avoid that:

- Think of your audience as the friend not the enemy, regardless of how aggressive they are.

- Take the first step in starting a friendly exchange with them, even if they are the ones who started the aggression.

- Avoid responding with sharp and direct statements. Keep the situation calm and don't respond in a patronising tone.

By doing that, you can intimidate the biggest bully without taking any action which justifies his or her behaviour.

In conflicts, be positive and seek a solution. Avoid being defensive as this will feed further attacks.

It's alright to **disagree with your audience**. Respect them, so that they respect you, but don't be afraid to politely disagree with an idea, or say no to a proposition, provided you have a good reason for doing so.

Earning respect is a reward for being able to state your opinion and backing it up with a good argument. However, be careful not to become patronising and stubborn.

When faced with an audience of people who are very knowledgeable and have higher positions than yourself:

- Don't be put off by the fact that they might know more about the subject than you do; the chances are they won't.

- Make sure you show them your knowledge by addressing the key areas and avoiding 'bullshit'.

- Showing credibility without arrogance is good. If you start showing off, they have the capability of shrinking you to a much smaller size, so avoid doing that.

Allow yourself to **admit mistakes**. It is very easy for knowledgeable people to spot your mistakes. To err is human; don't try to justify the error or hide it. Your audience will forgive you if you can rectify the mistake. Take responsibility for it and don't blame it on someone else such as the person who prepared the slides.

 INVOLVING YOUR AUDIENCE

There are several ways in which the **audience can participate**. Whether on an individual basis or in groups, they can be involved in proving certain points or contributing to the content of your presentation.

Letting your audience participate in demonstrations helps to keep them interested in your talk and makes them take part in explaining a point.

If they do things by themselves they are more likely to remember the idea behind the demonstration.

There are several ways that you can involve the audience.

Asking questions, and requesting a show of hands, gets people to think about your ideas. Not all of the audience may participate but they will surely take a few seconds to think about it. Then you can provide them with the answer which will not go unnoticed.

Using a questionnaire is sometimes useful. Ask people to take a few minutes and answer questions on paper before or during the presentation. You may decide to collect these papers or simply get them to keep them. This makes the audience think hard about the main issues you want to cover in your presentation.

Handling questionnaires can be a delicate matter. To avoid problems, consider the following:

- Don't put too many questions on the questionnaires. Try to keep them to under five.

- Make the questionnaire short and phrase your questions according to the points you will be making in the presentation.

- If you want to show the results of a multiple choice type of questionnaire, get someone else to help you collect and process the answers.

- The use of electronic polling systems can help you get instant answers and on-screen analysis from your audience. Using this system, you can ask a question and get the audience to press a button or a device supplied to them. This only works with yes/no and multiple choice type questionnaires.

- Only use questionnaires when you feel they are necessary to prove a point and keep the audience interested. Things can go wrong and have the opposite effect, so don't over-do it.

The most effective and entertaining way of **involving the audience** is getting volunteers to participate in **live demonstrations** or to help the presenter **illustrate an idea**. However, demonstrations can be easily mishandled and may go wrong. Should you decide to give a live demonstration and involve the audience in it, use the following guidelines:

- Choose a volunteer who you feel would fit the part to be performed.

- Look out for those who appear uninterested in your talk and try to involve them.

- Keep your demonstrations simple. You don't want to confuse a volunteer on stage and embarrass him or her.

- All your demonstrations should be basic and well within the capabilities of your volunteers.

- A demonstration can involve an element of humour. This helps the audience remember a particular point as they can associate it with a humorous action.

- Be patient with your volunteer and start by asking their name and their affiliation (company, university, department, etc.).

- Try to keep some distance between you and the volunteer, respecting their personal space.

- Get someone to explain any practical details to the volunteer on the side, before they are on stage.

- After the demonstration, make sure you thank them for their participation.

- Some demonstrations are given to smaller groups and they do not require volunteers. Make sure that you rehearse them beforehand and that everything you need is there.

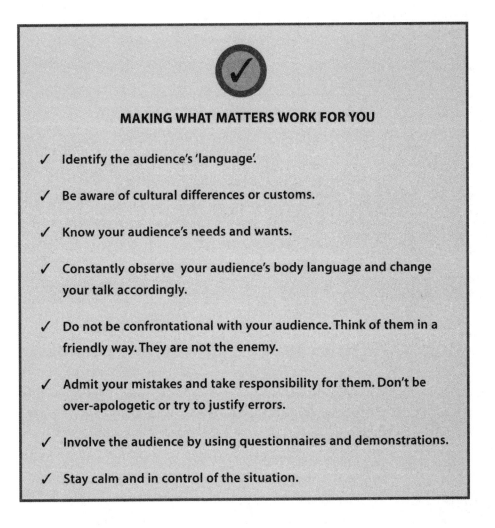

MAKING WHAT MATTERS WORK FOR YOU

✓ Identify the audience's 'language'.

✓ Be aware of cultural differences or customs.

✓ Know your audience's needs and wants.

✓ Constantly observe your audience's body language and change your talk accordingly.

✓ Do not be confrontational with your audience. Think of them in a friendly way. They are not the enemy.

✓ Admit your mistakes and take responsibility for them. Don't be over-apologetic or try to justify errors.

✓ Involve the audience by using questionnaires and demonstrations.

✓ Stay calm and in control of the situation.

7 Putting it all Together

Putting it all together is a juggling act.
You have to go on no matter what happens.

4

things that
really matter

1 **SETTING THE ENVIRONMENT**

2 **DEALING WITH STAGE FRIGHT**

3 **PRODUCING A CHECKLIST**

4 **SURVIVING UNEXPECTED PROBLEMS**

Now that you have tools and techniques to deliver a good presentation, it is time to put everything together in an excellent performance. No matter what you think of presentations, always **treat them as a small performance**. Performing in front of an audience involves not only you but your **surroundings** as well. The stage has a great effect on theatrical performances and so does the room in which you are presenting.

The visual aids you use play an essential role in the success of your presentation, and their use should be planned as the use of lighting and special effects is planned for a play.

As with all performances, 'stage fright' and things going wrong are common. Your role should be to reduce their impact by being well prepared. Your audience should not feel that something has gone wrong and should not know what goes on behind the scene. This is the magic in theatre and it should be so in presentations.

IS THIS YOU?

● *I need to show the executive committee our new promotional video and I'm not sure if we have a VCR.* ● *I'm going to use my computer and a data projector to give my presentation. I don't know what to do if something goes wrong.* ● *I'm presenting at a customer location next week and I have no idea what media are at my disposal.* ● *I do my preparation well, but I still feel extremely nervous when I present, I just can't help it.*

① SETTING THE ENVIRONMENT

The **environment** in which you present should reflect the importance of the occasion. It should be **customised to suit your presentation and style** so that it makes you feel confident.

Choosing the right place is an important first step. there are several types of venues in which you may give a presentation, from a small room to a large lecture theatre to an exhibition stand. You may not always find the perfect environment, but you should always try.

For a good venue, a room should have the following characteristics:

- **Large enough** to fit all the people invited or expected to attend.
- **Temperature control** is working properly and the ambient temperature is moderate and not too warm.
- All the **seats** are positioned in such a way that no one has to break their neck in order to see you or your visual aids.
- **Enough space** for visual aids and equipment.
- The **lighting** is controllable or at the right level for your projected slides to be seen.

- The room has enough **power points** located close to the electrical equipment you need to use, or enough extension leads.

- The **acoustics** are suitable for the presentation. Too much echo is not what you want. In larger rooms, the use of a microphone might be appropriate.

If you have a chance to go into the room some time before the presentation, look out for aspects that you can improve to fit the above criteria. For instance, if the ventilation is not suitable, try to change the temperature settings. Remember that an empty room feels different from a full one. Keep in mind the likely reactions of the people who will be there for your presentation.

Take a good look at the room and **customise the environment**. Check the following environmental aspects and act accordingly.

- If you notice that there is a clock on the wall which can be seen by the audience, try to hide it or remove it altogether. This is because people tend to look at the time and feel that it is not passing quickly enough.

- Close any windows that overlook a busy street to avoid noise pollution in the room. If the room is too warm and you feel the need to open a window, do so before the presentation and close it just before you start.

- If the room is small, with an elevated platform for the presenter to stand on, arrange the seating to give you enough space in front of the platform. Use this space and avoid standing at a higher level than the audience. This can only intimidate them and increase the barrier between you.

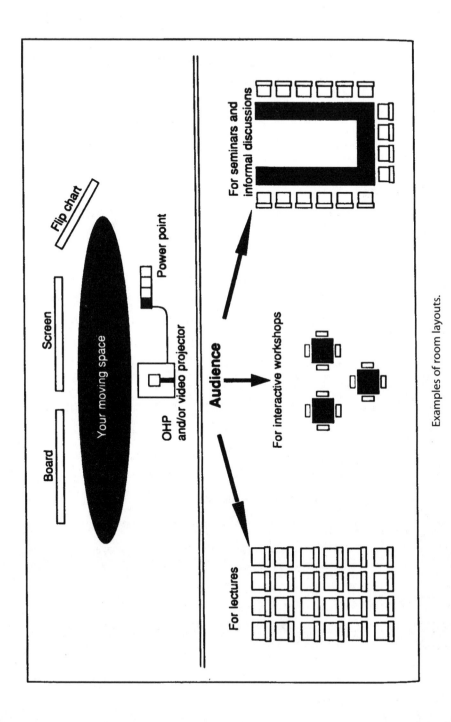

Examples of room layouts.

- In large lecture theatres, make sure that the lighting is controlled, so that when you start your presentation it is dimmed in the audience section. This helps the audience focus on you and your visual aids, as opposed to each other. However, it shouldn't be totally dark so that the audience can still make notes if they want to.

② DEALING WITH STAGE FRIGHT

Stage fright is suffered by most people in the spotlight, including actors, television presenters, public speakers and even politicians. It may not be apparent to us when we watch them, but they all experience it at some point.

The very thought of speaking in public may frighten some people. When the nervousness and the rush of adrenaline get out of control, the effects can be disastrous, but if controlled they can improve a presenter's performance.

The **symptoms of stage fright** can be felt in several ways:

- your neck and shoulders may feel stiff
- your mouth may be dry, or the very opposite
- you may feel nauseous
- your heart may beat faster and, to you, louder.

No matter how frightening the symptoms are, they can be helpful.

Many well-known public speakers and actors use their nervousness to give memorable performances. They are able to channel all the nervous energy into their performance.

There are two main types of cure for stage fright: **mental** and **physical**.

By having **the right frame of mind** you can overcome the effects of stage fright.

Points which can help you control your nervousness:

- Prepare well for your presentation and rehearse enough times to become confident. If you are comfortable with all the ideas you are presenting you will have overcome a major contributor to stage fright.

- Spend a few moments before the presentation visualising it in your mind, reviewing its structure and the key messages.

- If you are not reading from a script or note cards, have a written summary of the main points ready and at a short distance from you to use if needed. Even if you don't use it, the thought of it there is relaxing.

- No matter how nervous you feel, most of the symptoms will be apparent to you only and not the audience.

- Remember that the audience share your fear of public speaking and they are on your side. Even those who disagree with you still want to be stimulated and challenged by the content of your presentation.

- If you're not getting a reaction from the audience, this may indicate they are taken by your presentation. Don't get nervous thinking that they are not picking up anything you say.

Have something nice to look forward to after the presentation, to relax and avoid an anti-climax after a good performance. Take note of what worked for you so that you can use it next time.

The **physical aspects** of stage fright may be dealt with by doing the following:

- Relax your muscles. Go from your neck to your feet warming up each muscle in turn. Give yourself some time to relax before the presentation. Warm muscles can cope better with tension.

- Run through some of your speech, exercising your vocal chords by changing the volume and pitch. Exercise your facial muscles by exaggerating your facial expressions, as you go through parts of your talk.

- Take a deep breath from the level of your stomach and breathe out slowly. Repeat that a few times.

Channelling the nervous energy into your presentation will make you come across as enthusiastic and energetic. Remember that stage fright symptoms are mainly apparent to you and not to your audience.

 PRODUCING A CHECKLIST

Like a pilot before a flight, you need to have a **checklist** to remind you of what you have to do before your presentation. There are two types of checklists:

1. For a day or two prior to the presentation, to be used in the preparations for the delivery day.

2. For the day on which the presentation is taking place, to be used a few hours before the presentation starts.

Some items are on both lists, to make sure that they are not forgotten.

The **preliminary checklist**, which should be used a day or two before the presentation, will include some of the following items:

- Slides are ready and printed on transparencies.

- Any equipment is ordered.

- Rehearsals are finalised if not yet completed.
- If using a video, it is forwarded to the required position.
- A final estimate of the number of attendees is obtained.
- If applicable, a demonstration is tried and rehearsed. All required materials available.
- All the necessary arrangements are made for the room or hall to be used.
- You know where the venue is and you know how long it takes you to get there.
- Any support notes are printed and ready for handing out.

On the day of your presentation, try to arrive at least one hour before the start, to have enough time to go through your checklist. If there are some items which you cannot check off, estimate their effect on your presentation. If it is not too critical, ignore them.

The **checklist for the day** should include the following:

- You are dressed for the occasion.
- All the slides are complete and in order.
- All the equipment that you need is in the room and properly set up.
- Any electrical appliances that you are using are operational.
- Power points are positioned conveniently close to the equipment.
- If you are using a flip chart, check if it has enough pages for you to use.
- If you are using a board, make sure you have the appropriate writing materials.
- A suitable pointer for every visual aid is available.

- If reading from cards, make sure that they are in order.

- For live demonstrations, make sure that what you need is available and ready to use quickly.

- Make sure that you have the means of telling the time (clock at the back of the room, watch, etc.).

- A glass of water is available next to you in case you need it.

- If you want members of the audience to help you in demonstrations, you might want to talk to them beforehand.

- Supporting notes and handouts are with you.

- No barriers are present between you and the audience.

- If applicable, the sound system is operational and at the right level.

- Any lighting arrangements are agreed with the lighting assistant available on the day.

As you prepare for the presentation, keep a notebook next to you to write down other personalised items you may want to include in your checklist.

 SURVIVING UNEXPECTED PROBLEMS

You may find yourself in a situation where, in the middle of a presentation, something does not go according to your plan. To deal with this kind of situation, try the following:

- Always be prepared for the worst and don't leave anything to chance.

- Have an alternative plan to use if the original one fails.

- Be prepared to give your presentation without, or with different, visual aids. The equipment may break down in the middle of the presentation.

- Prepare alternative visual aids. This is particularly important if you are using a data projector or an older computer view panel. Some of these tend to heat up and play all sorts of tricks. You can always revert to a more traditional technology, like printed slides.
- If you feel your demonstration is not going to work, abort it. It is better than taking a big risk.

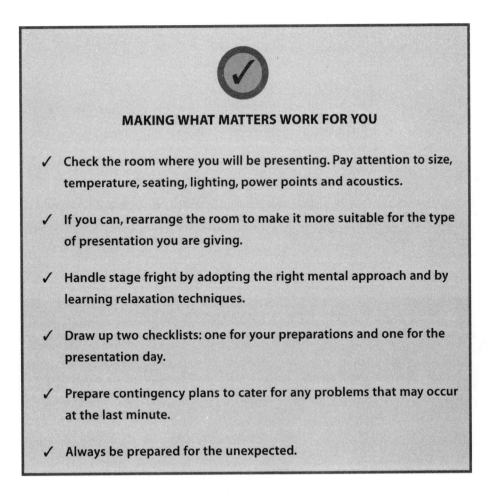

MAKING WHAT MATTERS WORK FOR YOU

✓ Check the room where you will be presenting. Pay attention to size, temperature, seating, lighting, power points and acoustics.

✓ If you can, rearrange the room to make it more suitable for the type of presentation you are giving.

✓ Handle stage fright by adopting the right mental approach and by learning relaxation techniques.

✓ Draw up two checklists: one for your preparations and one for the presentation day.

✓ Prepare contingency plans to cater for any problems that may occur at the last minute.

✓ Always be prepared for the unexpected.

Putting it into Practice

1. **Create your own style of communicating**
    - Communicate at the right level. Present your ideas as if you were telling a story.
    - Select the right style for the occasion – either formal or informal.
    - Use effective body language to make people feel at ease.
    - Be in control of yourself and of the situation.

2. **Prepare your presentation material**
    - Identify possible sources of information and research your subject thoroughly.
    - Decide what information you will use in the presentation. Don't cram too much information in.
    - Keep to the point. Classify the information according to what is essential, what is helpful and what would be good to include if you have time.
    - Make sure your script is well structured and uses appropriate language.

3. **Now plan your talk**
    - Draw a presentation layout, putting your ideas in the right sequence.
    - Tailor your introduction to your audience and memorise it. Reinforce the main points in the body of your presentation. Choose closing words that will make an impact on your audience.
    - Make effective use of the time you have to sell your ideas.
    - Decide whether you are going to *memorise* the

content of your presentation, read from a script or use notes.

4 **Enhance your presentation with visual aids**

- Use simple clear pictures to give your audience a clear visual representation of your thoughts.
- Use colour to add a professional finish to the presentation.
- Use a computer to either create slides or to give an on-screen presentation.
- Choose the right visual aids for the occasion.
- use notes and handouts to increase the impact of your presentation.

5 **Remember that speaking effectively can enhance the effectiveness of your presentation.**

- Develop an interesting voice by paying attention to tone, pitch, volume and clarity.
- Don't be afraid to use silence and pauses.
- Use stress and emphasis by changing pitch and adopting a decisive tone.
- Learn to project your voice appropriately.

6 *Manage your audience*

- Choose words your audience will understand.
- Find out what you can about your audience during the preparation stage.
- Read your audience's body language to spot signs of interest or lack of it.
- Avoid conflict and confrontation. Admit your mistakes and take responsibility for them.

- Involve your audience by using questionnaires and demonstrations.

7   Put everything together for a successful performance

- Customise your environment to suit your presentation and style.

- Use relaxation techniques if you suffer from nerves before your presentation.

- Draw up two checklists: one for your preparations and one for the presentation day itself.

- Prepare for the unexpected. Leave nothing to chance.